Theology
with a *Kiss*
Life In His Service

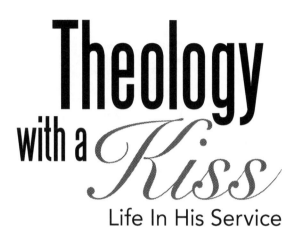

AL PAINE

WESTBOW®
PRESS
A DIVISION OF THOMAS NELSON
& ZONDERVAN

Scripture taken from the King James Version of the Bible.

Scriptures taken from the Holy Bible, New International Version®, NIV®. Copyright © 1973, 1978, 1984, 2011 by Biblica, Inc.™ Used by permission of Zondervan. All rights reserved worldwide. www.zondervan.com The "NIV" and "New International Version" are trademarks registered in the United States Patent and Trademark Office by Biblica, Inc.™ All rights reserved.

WestBow Press books may be ordered through booksellers or by contacting:

WestBow Press
A Division of Thomas Nelson & Zondervan
1663 Liberty Drive
Bloomington, IN 47403
www.westbowpress.com
1 (866) 928-1240

Because of the dynamic nature of the Internet, any web addresses or links contained in this book may have changed since publication and may no longer be valid. The views expressed in this work are solely those of the author and do not necessarily reflect the views of the publisher, and the publisher hereby disclaims any responsibility for them.

Any people depicted in stock imagery provided by Thinkstock are models, and such images are being used for illustrative purposes only. Certain stock imagery © Thinkstock.

ISBN: 978-1-4908-4212-7 (sc)
ISBN: 978-1-4908-4213-4 (e)

Library of Congress Control Number: 2014911284

Printed in the United States of America.

WestBow Press rev. date: 6/25/2014

Contents

Preface

Jesus loves me—this I know
Cause the Bible tells me so.
Little ones to him belong.
They are weak, but He is strong.

Yes, Jesus loves me—
Yes, Jesus loves me—
Yes, Jesus loves me—
The Bible tells me so.

This little hymn was sung by me and others in our early childhood days. It meant a lot to me back then that my God was watching over me and loved me individually and wanted me to be his forever (eternally).

I honestly believe that the caring and compassionate Sunday school teachers that we had did their homework diligently and made sure that we as young persons understood the true meaning of God's Word (Bible).

I also believe that even though I didn't reach out to the Lord and accept him as my Savior until I was seventeen years old, he was indeed reaching out to me, a young Sunday school child.

The more scholastically theologians (studiers of the Bible) call this *revelation*. The whole intent of this writing is to make the simple truth of the Bible identifiable (understandable) to the fifth-grader or the senior citizen. In this endeavour I pray that the Lord will guide me in the Holy Spirit and truth, declaring to you the reader what the Lord wants you to understand about the Word and his obvious love for you.

Introduction

If I didn't believe that the Lord loves me and that he didn't love you as well, it would be totally absurd (ridiculous) for me to even start the process of writing this book.

You will note that many times in the text I will undergo this analysis:

- process (wiring)
- revelation (reveal)
- Word (Bible and/or Jesus)
- forever (eternally)

The reason for this is not to make the reader feel uncomfortable about the reading but to make sure that the emphasis of the message is aimed at a fifth-grade level of reading and is understandable to the senior citizen.

One underlying factor (reason) for my writing this book has come about as the result of two different circumstances that happened to society and me in particular in my lifetime.

Firstly I was what you would call a Bible pusher for a few years. I belonged to a group of people called the Gideons. Every year we would go to the public schools and distribute New Testaments to fifth-grade students.

I don't remember exactly when (although it could be researched), but at some point the government stopped the Gideons from going to the schools to distribute our New Testaments to the students.

Not only did the government stop the distribution of the Bible (New Testament) within the schools, but they also demanded that the Gideon Bibles be removed from public places like hotels (like the Sheraton) and motels (like Best Western).

Eventually this stopped the Gideon movement in public places. I had moved from the area where I had first joined the Gideons, so eventually I dropped out of the organization altogether. I did not leave because it was not a good organization but because the government had already stopped what I felt was meaningful. It seemed that we were once reaching at least some young people to Christ.

The second reason for the writing of this book is also a personal dissatisfaction with what a majority of theological seminaries are presenting in their courses to the people who will be our future pastors, teachers, and scholars in the field of biblical study. I will address some of these problems later in this writing.

But first, let's start with what I believe is the Bible's most important concept (thought), and that's love.

Love

John 3:16 is probably one of the most read passage in Sunday schools, churches, Bible studies, etc. In fact, an independent recording artist by the name of Cindy Tucker has done one of the best renditions of this scripture in song. If you get the opportunity to hear this song, I am sure you will be truly blessed. Like me, Cindy belongs to a group of independent recording artists whom people can listen to free of charge on SongCastRadio.com.

Obviously God has shown his love for his creation (world and universe) as well as his creatures (humans) by sending his Son (Jesus) as a sacrifice for all of our sins. The Holy Scriptures state that if we believe in Jesus as the Son of God and confess him as such, we have already been saved by grace through the Spirit revealing this truth to us, and we have already passed from death to life.

Scripture also affirms (makes known to us) that if we confess that we acknowledge (or make known) our sins and ask Christ to come into our hearts, we have already been judged. When we lived without Jesus in our hearts, we were condemned to judgment, but now that we have been accepted as adopted sons and daughters of God, we are no longer condemned. This is very important. We are human, and therefore, we are weak. Satan (the Devil) knows this and wants us to turn people away from God. He is a clever deceiver. There is no truth in him, and he wants to destroy as many of us as he is able to do. We, however, have a mediator (speaker for us) to God, namely Christ, the Son of God, and when we do sin, we should immediately confess our sins to Jesus and ask forgiveness (cleansing us from our sins) and a renewed spirit to be within us.

You see, once we belong to God, that doesn't mean we won't sin. We are *human*! Unfortunately humans make a lot of mistakes. We should obviously try to live as sinless a life as possible, but when we do make mistakes, Jesus is the one to turn to.

I believe I mentioned earlier that I accepted Christ as my Savior when I was seventeen. I am now seventy years old and can assure you that I have made many mistakes in life and have sinned more than I want to think about. However, when I do think about my past mistakes, I often turn to Psalm 51, where David writes, "Create in me a clean heart, O God, and renew a right Spirit within me." KJV There is much more to this psalm. After David had sinned against the Lord, he penned this particular psalm. I urge you to find it in your Bible and read it, considering how this psalm could even relate to your own present situation.

Once you have considered any passage of Scripture as being an accurate description of your present situation, place yourself in prayer to the Lord with the Spirit's leading and feel the presence of the Lord as he lifts that burden from your soul.

God (the Father) mentioned to Moses long ago on Mt. Sinai that he was God, the only God to be worshipped, and that the people should love him with all their hearts. In giving Moses what is known as the Ten Commandments, God also states that we should love our neighbours as ourselves.

Obviously love was important to God then and indeed is still important to him today. Jesus recaptured this Spirit when he told his disciples that the two greatest commandments were these two described above. At least one of the apostles indicated in Scripture that love covers a multitude of sins.

Thinking along these lines, I can assure you that I feel very blessed to be able to be called a son of God. Here is why! Jesus was asked in Scripture, "Lord, how many times must I forgive my brother—seven times a day." Jesus answered back, "Not seven but seventy times seven." Math 18;22 That's a lot of forgiveness, and I wouldn't dare count how many times I have had to ask the Lord's forgiveness for sins in my life.

There have been times in my life (and probably yours as well) when I have felt that no one cared for me and wondered what might happen to me. This feeling could come during a financial matter where the outlook was dismal (difficult to correct). It could come in a relationship where a spouse or friend left with no reason except that it was just not working out. We live in a very impersonal world today, and it carries over even in these situations. It might even come during the loss of a loved one when it seems as if the world is caving in on you.

Remember that in any of the previously described situations, Jesus loves you and is always there for you. You only have to reach out to him and say a simple prayer like this: "Lord Jesus, I know you care for me and you can see the mess I'm in. Please help me to have more faith and trust in you to see me through this difficult time in my life."

Trust in Jesus to indeed see you through these situations. However, remember that he is holy. It is not always possible. For instance, when you are in or come upon a terrible accident and you confront the Lord, you may be laid out on the ground. He will still hear your prayer, and I'm sure he will respond as he is able. But in your own privacy when you are able, get down on your knees and pour yourself out to the Lord, and he will bless you in more ways than you can imagine.

First of all you have honored the holiness of our Lord. Secondly you have asked sincerely for his help in your time of trouble, and thirdly he loves you. With this relationship between you and God, how can the Devil or the world overtake you? You belong to God, and he is very concerned about your well-being. The Scripture says that God is a jealous God. He may allow bad things to happen, but he will not let his own be destroyed by evil. Evil does exist, but it has a short life span. When you belong to God, your life span is eternal. Have faith and follow the Lord's directions. If you are God's follower, this world will never be your home. As the old hymn proclaims,

> This world is not my home.
> I'm just a passing through.
> If heaven is not my home,
> O Lord, what will I do?

The angels beckoned me
from heaven's open door.
And I won't feel at home
in this world evermore.

In closing, may the love of God, the salvation of the Lord Jesus, and the illumination of the Spirit be with you and yours. May your hearts be filled with love for your God and your neighbors. It is the scriptural thing to do, and besides, you belong to God. He loves you and deserves your love flowing back to him.

God bless you in your life with the Lord.

Idolatry

In the *Bible Dictionary, idolatry* is defined as the worship of something created as opposed to worshipping the Creator. God is the Creator, and we are the creation of his divine authorship. Humans are God's highest level of creation, for we are made in his image. Although he formed and molded everything else in the universe, humankind is unique and bears God's image.

God's requirement for humankind since day one has been to worship him and him alone. We are to have no other gods before him to worship and bow down to, no idols made of any material, no worship of the sun, moon, and stars. Nothing else that God created is to be worshipped as we live our lives out in this world.

When we bow down to anything other than God, we are worshipping idols. We are replacing our Creator with a man-made object or something else that God created for our well-being, not for our worship. The sun, moon, and stars are mentioned as entities that people have made into their gods over the centuries of being on this earth. Anything that replaces God in the mind of the worshipper is an idol.

Many of us who go to the theaters to see the latest movie are in danger of making a particular actor or actress an idol and worshipping him or her as we might worship God. Let's say that you like action movies, that Tom Hollywood is your favorite actor, and that you won't go to any movie unless he is in it. You may wind up worshipping Tom Hollywood more than you do God.

Or let's say you have a favorite car—maybe a Ford Thunderbird, for instance—and you won't buy any other car but a Ford Thunderbird. Because you are wealthy enough to afford many of these vehicles, you have a collection of six or more of these cars, and they have become what you worship. In this case the Thunderbird has replaced God and become your idol.

I have personally had friends who are never satisfied with a particular home they own. They seem to be purchasing bigger and better homes every three to four years. If it's bigger, better, and more expensive, it becomes a need for these people to acquire this new home. When a house replaces God, it becomes that person's idol.

The same thing could be said of sports, hobbies, jewelry, or anything else that would take an individual's mind off God and would see that person worship the idol he or she has made. It could also come in the form of employment—always looking for that better job. It could come in the form of education—never learning enough but wanting more. It could even come in the form of clothing. For instance, if you wear Levi jeans, you may find that you are part of the "in group." But if you don't wear Levi jeans, you may feel like a nobody.

These are all idols and have replaced worshipping God with the worship of material things.

This type of worship goes against the very first commandment God gave to the people of Israel. "You shall have no other Gods but me. I alone am God." The question is this: What makes a person reject God and replace him with an idol? I personally believe that having the free will to choose what you want to do or decide what gives you the most pleasure or what gives you more honor among your peers and lifts you high above the rest is a good part of the problem of replacing God with idols.

When God created mankind, he commanded Adam and Eve not to eat from the Tree of Knowledge of which gave them the knowledge of good and evil. The Devil tempted Eve, and she saw that the fruit was pleasant to look at and great to eat. Furthermore, this knowledge, she thought, might make her more like God, so this became her idol. Sin prevailed, and God was put out of mind until he came looking for Adam and Eve in the garden. Once God found them, he knew that he had his redemptive work cut out for him.

The Devil and told the woman that surely God wouldn't kill them, that they would not die, and he was right. God did not kill them but actually made clothes for them to cover the nakedness that they discovered after they ate the forbidden fruit. What the Devil didn't suggest, however, was that God would permanently banish them from the garden and make work and childbirth difficult for them all of their days. They no longer had the personal relationship that had existed with God before their fall. Paradise wasn't to be their home any longer.

Because of the fall all of mankind became sinners in need of redemption, for mankind took the free will discussed earlier and chose to replace God and his sovereignty (control) over their lives. What was paradise became a living hell on earth. Idol worship has been a real problem down through the ages and continues to be a thorn in the Lord's side to this very day.

Idolatry has a very vicious side to itself. It has taken many young and old people alike and made them slaves to drugs, alcohol, sex, profanity, you name it. In the news every day we see how movie stars or rock stars or even teachers have influenced young lives into doing things wrong because they have become the young people's idols. Many times these relationships have brought tragedy to households across North America, young people committing suicide or overdosing, severely damaging their brains and leaving them in vegetative states (brain dead). Many of the actors and rockers have come to end their own lives with substance abuse and have committed suicide themselves. You will find circumstances like these in your newspapers and on the TV screens quite frequently. The real tragedy is that they have left society with a mess to fix up. Broken homes and broken dreams have all come about because God had been replaced with an idol.

How does society handle the problem? Most of the time governments make stiffer laws and penalties for using and selling drugs, etc. Does it solve the problem? Most of the time, *no!* Not much is really accomplished at all! The jails may be full, and the victims may be temporarily satisfied with the judicial actions; however, God is still out of the picture. Mankind hasn't taken the time to search into scripture to see how God would want these situations handled.

What is really needed is for God to become real in people's lives. He must become the one that individuals worship. He must be given the glory, honor, and praise that he deserves. It is my hope that many of you who read these lines will give God complete control of your lives and get rid of all your idols.

An idol is what it is—an idol, something generally fashioned by mankind, not something to be worshipped by anyone.

God is who he is, Creator of the universe, the loving Father, holy, one to be feared (yet loved), one to be honored and obeyed, and most of all, one to be worshipped by us all, everyone from the poorest to the richest, from the youngest to the oldest, men and women of all walks of life, all races. Love the Lord, your God, with all your being.

Some biblical perspectives concerning idols are worth summarizing here. Greed is considered a form of idolatry and is condemned by the Scriptures. Sometimes it seems funny when you hear a little one say to his or her mom or dad, "I want that. I want that." This is a form of greed, if left totally unchecked, can lead to a more serious problem later in the child's life. If children get everything they say they want, then it becomes important that they continue to get exactly what they want when they want it later on in life. One statistic that was recently brought to my attention was that one third of all teenagers in Canada have a criminal record a mile long by the time they are eighteen years old. I personally believe that because young people are not charged or held accountable for their actions and only get their hands slapped when they find themselves in serious trouble is the cause of this whole mess judiciously.

Money is another false God and another idol to many. One good example of this problem is the lotto system. Every day one can play the lotto in some form or another. Why do people play? To get rich quick—that is their hope. Some people have been known to literally gamble their homes and lives away, all because they may hit the "big one" or their ship is "just around the corner."

The New Testament states specifically that idolaters have no inheritance in the kingdom of God. And why wouldn't this be so! Greed, money, and gambling have become the idolaters' God. God is absent from all of their thoughts.

Idols cannot save an individual. An idol cannot make sacrifices for your sins. Jesus has become the sacrifice for your sins in his death on the cross. He died for your sins and mine. Flee from your idols and ask the Lord Jesus to help you get rid of all your idols and false gods. If asked, he will come into your heart and help you overcome your weaknesses. He has to be asked. Ask him, feel his presence, and be free from your idols.

I pray for those of you facing this problem of idols. I know what it is to suffer from idol worship. I have struggled with what many of you may be struggling with now. It isn't easy giving up something you enjoy doing and want to do. However, when you are consumed by an idol of any sort, you are not worshipping the true God. You must let God have control of your life and trust in his releasing you from the bondage you find yourself in.

If you hear an inner whisper in your ear and if it is God saying, "Come worship me. I am your God and deserve your worship of me alone," let him come into your life and cleanse you of all your sins. He loves you and only wants your love in return.

Fear

Godly fear is a feeling of reverence, awe, or respect. It is also the healthy side of fear. The Scripture also declares that "the fear of the Lord is the beginning of knowledge" (Proverbs 1:7) as well as "the beginning of wisdom" (Proverbs 9:10).

On the other hand, harmful fear is a sense of terror or dread. A harmful fear is an unpleasant emotion caused by a sense of danger. The Holy Scriptures also indicate that the wicked constantly fear someone or something because their lives are out of order (not right with God).

For instance, a bank robber who successfully pulled off a robbery at a bank is in constant fear of the people who may recognize him from surveillance cameras or photos taken while the robbery was taking place. He will have a constant fear of anyone in uniform representing the police or security forces because they may be looking for him. Instead of being able to walk down the street with his head held high, he will duck into corners and walk down side streets, always hiding and afraid to come out in the open. He has now taken on a criminal role in life and will constantly fear being caught and put in jail or killed by a police officer. His world now is one where he is totally on the run from anything to do with law and order. His life is now in chaos, completely out of control, and he doesn't know which way to turn next.

The bank robber's fear has certainly come about because of his sin of robbing the bank. Whatever the reasons he had for robbing the bank in the beginning, his crime has now escalated into a nightmare (or horrible) experience. Everyone becomes an enemy, particularly those in authority (police) and possible witnesses to the crime. Because of this sin, he has alienated himself from his family, friends, acquaintances, and society as a whole. He doesn't realize it yet, but he won't really be free from fear until he is caught and put in prison for his crime. If he survives being caught, he will have a long time to consider his actions in a correctional institution. Hopefully while he is in prison, he will hear the Word of God and decide to turn his life over to Christ by trusting in him and accepting him as his Savior and Lord.

This situation is not totally uncommon for someone who has committed this type of crime. These people can be totally changed while they are serving time in prison for their crimes.

Of course, he may still be fearful about what the future may bring. He might also fear what others may say about him when he is released from prison or what they might even do to him. And of course, the law (authorities) will always be looking over his shoulder to make sure that he isn't involved with criminal activities or criminals of any nature.

If our bank robber does accept Christ as his Savior while he is in jail, he will be able to conquer a great deal of the fears that he has by completely trusting in God for his future. He obviously would have been better off if he had done that in the beginning; however, sin blinded him to that fact, and he only saw his need to rob the bank at that time.

He now has a new life ahead of him by obeying God's will in his life. God will be his refuge, even if he has lost his friends, family members, jobs, etc. By trusting in God's provision, he will be on the right road to recovery from the mess that sin had gotten him into initially (in the beginning). If our bank robber fears the Lord reverently, he will find that his needs will be provided for. He will be blessed with new friends and work, and he will also be restored to society. God will protect him from those fears that damaged his life in the past. His life has now changed for the better, and he will be able to serve the Lord by having the right kind of fear to govern his life.

The sin of alcoholism is another area that brings many people (men and women) down in life. The average alcoholic (in the beginning) has no fear of anything whatsoever. Alcoholics live in a constant state of denial. They can handle their own drinking problems—or so they think. In fact, they will tell you in no uncertain terms that they *do not have a drinking problem.* Generally this denial will go on until it cost them their jobs, families, social status, friends, and associates and eventually lands them in jail usually because of a car accident, an assault, or some other recklessness that "pushed them over the edge." In some of the most severe cases alcoholics will still deny they have a drinking problem even after they are locked up in jail. It generally takes a severe action like killing one of their family members or almost killing themselves in an accident to help alcoholics realize that they have a real serious problem.

Unfortunately alcoholism like other drugs is difficult to overcome. Once a person is addicted, it becomes a lifetime struggle to control the addiction. The first step, of course, is admitting that the addict indeed has a problem that has to be dealt with. Secondly one must follow a step-by-step program of detoxifying one's system and avoid further drug abuse. Thirdly the person must take one day at a time. Every day away from the addiction is a victory for the addict. The support of family and friends is very important to helping one overcome this horrible sin. Also, if the individual has come to Christ as the bank robber did, his or her chances of success will be that much greater with God's intervention.

In my seventy years on this earth, I have never known a bank robber. In my family and among my friends I have known of some drug or alcohol addicts and have learned about the horrible situations they have found themselves in. I can only imagine; however, I don't know this experience myself. I would think that many of them have found themselves suffering from terrible feelings of fear. Some have gone so far as to try to commit suicide. Sf course, some have succeeded in doing just that. It must be horribly depressing to get to the point in life where one thinks the only way out is suicide.

In either of these cases there is no easy fix. Yes, if the individuals involved had had God in their lives, they probably wouldn't have ended up the way they did. That doesn't mean that their lives would have been easy and without problems, but it does mean that they would have a higher power looking out for their interests here on earth. The odds are that out of respect and fear of God, their individual problems wouldn't have allowed them to escalate to such disastrous points.

As individuals, we do not know how our lives will turn out. God, however, knows our every move, and he allows us the free will to do as we please.

We should try our best, however, to please our Creator, for he cares for us more than we will ever know. He will always love us. To God, we will always be humans—even in eternity. We may be perfected humans; however, we will be human, and that's all there is to that. We will never be divine!

If as you are reading this book and you feel you are in need of the Lord's presence in your life, I pray that you drop to your knees and pour out your heart's desires to the Lord and let him go to work in your life. I can assure you that he is only a prayer away. And he wants to hear from you. He may answer your prayer right away, or it may take some time for your requests to be answered. But remember this—the Lord's timing is always right. In this world we may become very impatient with what is going on around us. God, on the other hand, has been very patient with us all, and we should strive to be more like him.

My wife and I had a tremendous fear, and a feeling of depression hit us head on after about a year into our marriage. My Vietnamese mother-in-law had been hit by a motorcycle and literally dragged three blocks in the city of Saigon. She was not expected to live very long, and the family was preparing here as well as in Saigon for her eventual funeral. At that time my wife and I couldn't afford to immediately give up our jobs and go to Saigon to visit her mother. The financial stress alone would have been overwhelming for both of us. However, we had God in our lives, and he was an intricate part of our relationship. As soon as we saw our problem in black and white (financial/individual terms) and in God's light (spiritual terms), we both went to our bedroom, got down on our knees, and prayed to God that he would be kind enough to spare this beautiful old Vietnamese lady and perform one of his miracles in her life.

Praise the Lord! Our heavenly Father did exactly that! Mother was brought out of a comma, bandaged up, and treated for wounds, and within a week she was sent home to her family in Saigon. My wife and I don't talk very often about this situation, but believe me—it was real. I have had the opportunity to visit my mother-in-law twice since that accident, and each time has been a blessing to me. She is a tough old Christian lady and loves her Lord immensely. We know that we may not see her again before she dies of old age. (She is now eighty-nine.) However, we are very grateful to the Lord for his allowing us the opportunity to enjoy our mother that much longer on this earth. Please don't let anyone *ever* tell you that God is out of miracles, for that is not so! Every breath we take is another miracle from God. Think about that!

Education

Education as defined in the *Bible Dictionary* is simply the transfer of knowledge, morals, and attitudes from one person to the next.

In Old Testament times the goal of education was to prepare people to know God and to live peacefully with one another. Children were taught at home by their parents, the father being most responsible for making sure that his children were properly educated.

Educating the children was considered a never-ending task. The mother played the most significant role in educating the children in the early years. Until a young man could join his father in the field or workshop, he would receive instruction from his mother in the home. It was the parents' duty and responsibility to instruct their children, and this responsibility continued until death.

It wasn't until New Testament times that reading, writing, and arithmetic were introduced in synagogues and schools established for learning. God was the model for proper teaching. God was the master teacher who taught by the Word and example. Formal education started at the age of six or seven and continued until about twelve years of age. If the parents wanted a son to receive more training, he was sent to the city where a number of notable rabbis had schools. Usually all the kids were taught in a one-classroom atmosphere. The students were at different levels of knowledge, so the education of each was individualized, allowing for each student to progress as he was able.

The law of the Lord, the Holy Scriptures, and general knowledge and wisdom were the areas of education taught in these schools. Knowing Jesus Christ, living to fear the Lord, and showing him reverence were fundamental.

Obviously the purpose of education was to first teach the information needed to inspire holy living, to gain skills in holy living, and to prepare the student for adulthood. Much of the lesson assignments were spoken out loud so that the student might memorize the lesson as he read.

As time went by, education became governed by local, state, or provincial governments quite like we have today. More scientific and secular issues have been brought into the classrooms to influence the pupils' thoughts and personalities.

God was replaced by the influence of evolution forced on students by the educational systems. In the United States, atheists fought and won in the court that the Lord's Prayer be removed from public schools. When I was a young student, we always recited the Lord's Prayer and said the Pledge of Allegiance to our country's flag. One atheist changed all that, which is certainly a victory for Satan and his angels. Not long after that even the Pledge of Allegiance to one's flag was taken out of the schoolroom's morning activities. So in effect, respect of God and respect of one's nation was taken away from future students' education.

In the early 1930s the theaters in the United States introduced homosexuality for the first time on film. Sexual perversion had entered into the field of education. Therefore, it became acceptable in theaters and society. Certainly since then and particularly since the early 1970s one can hardly find a film that does not have some sexual message or overtone in its presentation to the public. The message now is that if you are gay, it's okay, and that message has now completely taken over Hollywood and the majority of its productions. Sex is life, and if you are not having it, something is wrong with you—or so Hollywood says.

In the midsixties I was accepted to a prestigious acting school in New York. My family owned a property by a summer theater, and we had gotten to know several prominent actors and producers at the time. I had not discussed my application to this school with my mother and father until I was formally accepted. But when I did tell my parents that I had been accepted and the school was awaiting my entrance into the first year of acting school in New York City, *oh boy!*

My parents gave me a lecture that I will never forget. First I had not even told them that I was applying for the school. Secondly I was under the age of eighteen, graduating from high school at sixteen and a half. Thirdly they were still in charge of my education, and I would not be going to acting school in New York City or anywhere else for that matter.

Though I didn't know it at the time, my parents assured me that the majority of Hollywood actors were either homosexual or lesbians and that some of them went

21

both ways. I certainly would not be allowed to associate with any of those kinds of people, let alone join them in movie productions. It wasn't until years later that I really started to believe what my parents had made known to me when I was a young person. I did, however, follow their example and join the US Air Force, and I stayed with the program for sixteen years. Through governmental support, I had received my bachelor's degree in education and my master's in orthotics at New York University.

During these years of my education I had seen many things and been exposed to many theories about what was right and what was wrong. I had been taught that if the government said it was okay, then it was indeed okay. This was indeed wrong, and as the preacher says in the book of Proverbs, "all is vanity."

The acceptance of homosexuality of any kind has invaded the home, the school, the community, and the government. This should not be so, but laws have even been made to make sure that these secular activities are protected by governing officials.

The *Bible Dictionary* defines a homosexual as a person who is attracted sexually to a member of his or her own sex. Homosexuality is prohibited in Scripture and was a major cause of divine judgement against Sodom and Gomorrah. God's wrath stands against such behavior, whether it is practiced by men or by women.

No wonder with Hollywood producing films and introducing homosexuality to the public and with the government sanctioning such behavior that the Lord's Prayer and the Pledge of Allegiance to the flag have been taken out of the classrooms.

The problem has gone full circle and is now filling theological seminaries with perverse instruction for ordaining homosexual and lesbian ministers and priest as well as professors claiming to be teaching the Word of God. This should not be so! Many feminists have used this strategy to go so far as to call God a she. Nowhere in Scripture do I find God as being a female. Jesus refers to God as his father. He talks about his father's house and not his mother's house.

Adam and Eve were created to procreate and fill the world with mankind. In his infinite wisdom God did not create Jill and Jane and say, "Fill the world with your offspring." He also did not create Bob and Joe and say, "Have yourself a jolly good time." Truly homosexuality has been a long-term problem for the Lord, and Satan has used it in the past as well as today to destroy many people made in the image of God.

The following are facts that were brought up on the Internet and are deemed reliable at this writing. It just goes to show how heavily Satan has used the homes, communities, and governments to introduce the form of education he wants society to get. His anti-Christian ways have put millions of dollars in the hands of those who pervert the Scriptures, prevent justice, and pervert human lives.

Here are the questions asked on Internet Explorer:

- How many Christians are involved with acting in Hollywood? There was no answer given.
- How many Hollywood couples are actually married? There was no answer given.

- How many people are in Canada? There are approximately 34,278,400.
- How many natives live in Canada? Approximately one million natives live in Canada.
- How many French people are in Canada? About 22.3 percent of the population is French.
- How many English people are in Canada? About 58.4 percent of the population is English.
- How many people in Canada watch pornography? About 70 percent of all men between the ages of eighteen to twenty-four watch pornography. One in three porn users are women. Sunday is the day most porn is viewed.
- How much pornography is viewed in the average home per week? In worst-case scenario people watch five hours of porn a day for five days per week.
- When did Facebook introduce online dating? In 2004, it was a two-billion-dollar industry.
- What percentage of criminals is jailed for sex offenses? About 25 to 30 percent off all offenses are sex-related.
- What percentage of criminals is in jail for alcoholism? About 50 percent of criminals are in jail because of alcoholism-related incidents at a cost of $100,000 per year per person.
- What percentage of criminals is in jail for drug-related offenses? British Columbia has the highest rate in Canada, showing 426 of 100,000 people, which makes the second national average.

- ○ How young might the girls of Nanaimo start to engage in sexual activity? Many start at least by the age of fourteen, and some start earlier.
- ○ How old are students before the schools introduce condoms to them? On average, they are between fifteen and seventeen years old.
- ○ When do most parents start their girls on birth control pills? Many start taking the pill between twelve and seventeen years of age.
- ○ How many homes in Nanaimo house unmarried couples? Approximate 14 to 15 percent of house have unmarried couples.
- ○ What is the divorce rate in Nanaimo? The divorce rate is more than 50 percent and climbing.
- ○ When did the government introduce sex education in schools? The Public Health Agency of Canada introduced a form of sex education in 2003.

If you are concerned about this problem at all, I suggest for you to get into the Holy Scriptures (the Word of God). Don't accept anything you know is wrong, and you can urge those you come in contact with to join you in prayer and concern. Assist them as best as you are able so that you can all rise above these problems.

Truly with the above statistics, you are able to see that Nanaimo is indeed in need of a spiritual overhauling. My prayer is that the churches speak out more emphatically to their congregations about these problems and this influence on our daily lives. To the churches, I suggest that it might be a good idea to occasionally hear inmates (under guarded circumstances) minister to the people about how their problemic path led them to jail, ruined their family, disrupted their lives, etc.

After seventy years of living I do not consider myself a naïve individual. I believe that young people are bombarded every day with something that has to do with sex in one form or another. For instance, quite often on the Internet, people come across nude pictures of favorite actors of actresses. Please don't tell me that kids are not looking at this stuff every day. Not only that, today on the home page of my browser, I found these statements to entice one to look at this garbage: "A look at the 10 sexiest places on Earth," "The sexiest cars of the year," "The ten most sexual actresses in Hollywood." Sex is a big seller. Many social media sites sell sex every day. Hundreds of women in Nanaimo are willing to take a women's husband for a one-night stand anytime, anyplace, anywhere.

In conclusion, we certainly have to do something to change our education process. If we cannot change the system, maybe God will allow us to be changed for his glory and his good. Pray with me … for change!

No matter what anyone tells you, you do not have to accept homosexuality of any kind. You may have to live around it, but you definitely do not have to accept it. I sometimes wonder how a man that turned to a homosexual relationship responds to his children—maybe something like this, "I am now your mommy, and the big guy over there is your daddy." Do you think that these children will turn out normal? No, they won't indeed. Homosexuality is not normal. It is sick.

The homosexual would like for you to believe that he or she was born that way, that it's in their genes. Give me a break! God doesn't make homosexuals! Their actions are sinful and self-willed, so the homosexual can blame no one but his or herself. I might add that because society has accepted this behavior, that the homosexual may also blame society for part of his or her problem.

I wonder if they will ask their parents on their way to hell when the last trumpet sounds why they didn't instruct them properly and why they allowed them to give themselves over to the Devil. Satan will deceive as many as possible between now and then because he knows his days are numbered and he wants as many as possible to join him in eternal damnation. When the roll is called up yonder, he will not be there!

Inspiration

The *Bible Dictionary* states that inspiration is a technical term for the Holy Spirit's supernatural guidance of those who received special revelation from God as they wrote the books of the Bible.

The Bible conveys the truth that God wanted his people to know and spread throughout the world. Therefore, the Bible is trustworthy, a guide for holy living mixed with numerous instructions on how to prepare for eternal life with God and his saints.

The biblical writers received their inspiration for writing the Bible in various ways. For instance, Moses spoke directly to God and received his instruction firsthand. Moses was responsible for writing the first five books of the Old Testament and giving instructions to the Israelites as to how God wanted them to live their daily lives and what he was expecting from his chosen people. Probably the first thing that most people associate Moses with is the Ten Commandments given to him on Mt. Sinai by the Lord God himself.

Angels spoke to other writers and passed on to them the information God wanted written down. John was instructed by God's angel throughout the writing of the book of Revelation, the last book of the Bible. He was shown some things that he was forbidden to write down. God has given mankind what he wants us to know about him, His kingdom, eternal life, etc. His words are authority. He intended for us to live by his words and to be holy as he is holy.

Other scriptures were written by inspiration from dreams or visions. Daniel comes to mind when one thinks about visions. He interpreted several dreams and visions that kings and others came to him about, for he was recognized as a man of God and respected for that knowledge that the Lord gave him.

Eyewitness accounts were those Scriptures written by the apostles in the Gospels of Matthew, Mark, and John. These individuals were men who walked and talked with the living God (Jesus Christ). Truly these men were everyday acquaintances with a very divine human being. Jesus gave all of mankindthe words of life and hope for eternal salvation through his death on the cross. God's redemptive plan is found in the Holy Scriptures from Genesis to Revelation.

Luke, on the other hand, was familiar with and in association with those individuals who were actual eyewitnesses of Jesus' miracles and teachings while he was on this earth. Luke put his gospel and the book of Acts together from thorough research and information gathered from these sources. Luke was obviously a very Christian man and was well educated based on his treatise. He traveled with Paul on many of Paul's missionary journeys and was introduced to much church planting as a result of these journeys. Indeed, the Holy Spirit inspired Luke to take into account this whole Christian movement and write his two treatises. Luke was concerned about informing his readers of the truths that were revealed to him through the Holy Spirit's intervention in his life.

The term *inerrancy* (without error) is used in the study of the Bible to make clear that we understand that these writers were under the influence of the Holy Spirit. And indeed these written accounts in Scripture where exactly what God wanted us to receive.

Another term that goes along with the idea of inerrancy is the word *infallibility* (not liable to fail). In other words, you can count on God's Word to be reliable in every way, shape, and form. His Word never fails and will always achieve what the Holy Father wants it to achieve.

Much Scripture that we read will be deemed historic because it describes things that happened in the past and gives the results of these happenings. Obviously these were written for those times but also should be used to give us an insight into how we today should live our lives. I mentioned redemption being important throughout Scriptures, but I will talk here about God's holiness. His holiness is talked about in all of the Holy Scriptures, and he challenges us to be holy by being more like Jesus in all that we do and say. Again we will never be perfect on this earth, but if we have the Lord on our side, we will never be defeated. We may suffer loss, setbacks, rebukes, etc., but we will triumph over all evil and temptation with the heavenly Father watching over us. I urge you at this point to ask the Lord into your heart now and accept Jesus Christ as your Lord and Savior. If you make this simple plea, he will do the rest and lead you to the paths of righteousness.

He will never let you down, and you will find that he is indeed the greatest friend you will ever have.

Salvation is the key to Scripture, and Jesus has made that salvation available to you and me. His shed blood is the atonement we need for forgiveness of sins, and the inspired writing by the prophets, apostles, and others have made that point very clear. When you read the Bible, read it meditatively (prayerfully) and ask God to make clear to you all that he wants you to know about a certain section or reading of Scripture that you have read. It may not be an immediate revelation, but you will be given your understanding as God allows. It may even take the form of a news item or climate condition or whatever, but God will reveal the intent of his Word to you as you are able to handle his truths. Trust in God, for he is trustworthy.

If you attend church on a regular basis, you will find another type of inspiration given in and coming from the Scriptures. Your minister has had to prepare his sermon to be delivered at your worship service by careful study of the Scriptures on the subject matter that he wishes to convey to the congregation. If you are blessed with a study Bible and other resources explaining Scripture, you will notice that some passages will have several lessons to be taught in a very concise portion of Scripture.

When you study Scripture, meditate on what you have read and ask God's guidance through the Holy Spirit to help you discover what he has inspired the writers to write. Ask the Lord for his help in your understanding of what the Scripture meant at the time it was written and how it applies to everyday life today. With careful, prayerful study habits, you will be rewarded with your searching the Scriptures for the truths that they reveal.

Let God's Word inspire you into living as holy of a life as you are able to live with the Spirit's guidance. Be holy because your God is holy. Don't be afraid to talk to him. He wants to communicate with you daily.

Name

A name is a label or designation that sets one person apart from another. For instance, my name is Alvino, and it was given to me by my mother and father in respect to the Italian family that had taken my father into their family when my dad lost his biological family. He grew up in New York City with his Italian brothers and sisters. My brother and sister also have Italian first names—Anthony and Audrey. We were known as the triple A's back east. Interestingly my name, Alvino, is used by the Italian people to designate first name, middle name, or last name. And I knew of a physician in Boston, Massachusetts, whose name was Alvino Alvino Alvino. Strange, eh? Most North Americans tend to name their children after a good friend, favorite family member, favorite movie star, etc. In my wife's Vietnamese culture, however, one is not allowed to name their children after a sister or close relative. At least that's how it was when she was born. It's changing today.

In biblical times there was a very important connection between the name of a person and what the name meant. For example, Issac measn laughter. His mother laughed at his birth Esau means hairy, and he was named that because of his appearance. Jacob means supplanter. He had grasped his brother's heel. Moses means *drawn out of the water.*

Some of the prophets like Isaiah and Hosea were given instructions by God as to what to name their sons and daughters.

Changing a name in the Bible was of great importance. God gave Abram the name of Abraham, meaning *father of many nations*. Jacob was given the name Israel, for he had struggled with God and man and had prevailed.

The Lord Jesus gave Peter (Cephas) this name to replace his old name Simon because he was the first to acknowledge that Jesus was indeed Lord and God. Jesus wanted the world to know that on the rock Peter, Jesus would establish his church.

All of us carry our own name but have the title Christian added to us if we have accepted the Lord Jesus as our Savior and our God. Other religions also have the names of their gods that they follow.

God revealed himself to Moses when Moses was staring at the burning bush on Mt Sinai as "I Am who I Am."

Mary was instructed by the angel to name her son Jesus, for he would be the Son of God. Zachariah was instructed by the angel in his vision in the temple to name his son John.

The apostle Paul describes Christians as people who name the name of the Lord. Paul also describes Jesus as being given the name above all names, a name that would be highly exalted.

Today the Lord isn't telling us what to name our children. Nor is he changing our names as was done with Abram, Jacob, and Simon. However, the Bible instructs us on how to honor the name of the Lord.

In Luke, we are told to rejoice about the fact that our names are written in the Lamb's Book of Life if we have accepted Jesus as our Savior and Lord and confessed such.

In Revelation, John explains that only those whose names are written in the Lamb's Book of Life will enter eternity with the Lord and Savior.

No matter what your name is, you are important to God. Jesus died on the cross for your and my salvation. If your name is in the Lamb's Book of Life, you will indeed enjoy eternal life and spend an eternity with your Lord and Savior, Jesus Christ.

Before we end this segment, let's look at what the Lord wants us to do with his name as well as what he doesn't want us to do with his name.

In the Old Testament, we are instructed not to misuse the name of the Lord. We are to exalt the name of the Lord and give him the glory due his name. We are to sing, praise, and glorify his name. And as Jesus instructed, his disciples in prayer we are directed to hallow his name.

Many people shy away from using the Lord's name at all; however, Jesus says call on the name of the Lord, and he will hear the pleas of a sincere heart. Call on the name of the Lord, and you will be saved.

The Lord Jesus also says, "Ask anything in His name and it will be done unto you." Believe in his name, and you will be saved, and your name will never be blotted out in heaven. What a glorious holy God who makes eternal life available to us all regardless of our names.

Remember this as well: At the name of Jesus every knee will bow and proclaim his as Lord and God. Scripture says it, so believe it!

Holy

As defined in the dictionary, *holy* is moral and ethical wholeness or perfection, freedom from moral evil. Holiness is one of the essential elements of God's nature required of his people. Holiness may also be rendered sanctification or godliness. The Hebrew word for *holy* denotes that which is sanctified or set apart for divine service. God calls us to be holy because he is holy. Jesus, Peter, and Paul all reiterate this fact in each of their ministries on this earth.

The Father, Son, and Spirit are all divine individuals/ beings. Everything about the Trinity is holy and should be treated as such by all of us. We are expected to be holy not on our own merit but through the Spirit that indwells in us. All Christians have been chosen and set apart to do God's will/service in our lives.

Although the world is Satan's present dwelling place, it still belongs to God. He was the Creator of all things, including this earth, and therefore where you meet Him—that piece of ground, sanctuary, stretch of road, group of people, friends, etc.—must be considered holy. The Spirit will guide and make God known to those who are chosen to serve the Lord.

Many stories have been recorded about soldiers on the battlefield coming to Christ in very horrific times. Others have come to Christ on their deathbeds. People like Corrie ten Bloom have been touched and led by God in the terrible setting of a concentration camp.

Some people have experienced an out-of-body experience and have been directed by the Spirit in what is expected of them after their spirits return to their bodies. Many of these experiences cannot be explained thoroughly by the human mind, but there are holy circumstances surrounding those who have had these experiences.

We live in what many call an ungodly world. And in many cases it seems as though that is a good charactization of the world today. However, never forget that a very holy God made this world and all that is in it. Because of his love for us and his creation, he sent his only Son into this world to be our Savior and Lord. He has never forgotten our framework. He created man from the dust, and to the dust we shall indeed return. However, the Spirit in us is a different matter. We have been chosen to do God's will on this earth, and he will have his way with each of us. Only by God's grace can we be considered holy. Without his grace imparted on us, we have absolutely no way of being holy or acceptable to God.

The Scriptures make it clear that it is by grace alone that we are saved and not by works. I agree with that, and yet I believe that we do have to work out our own holiness with the Spirit's help. I believe that there are degrees of holiness. Some of us will never get past the basic holiness stage of accepting Christ and his teachings.

We will be divinely blessed and guided by the Spirit, but because of our upbringing, social status, monetary wealth, etc., we become limited in the amount of holiness that we may achieve. Jesus teachings about the scribes and Pharisees point to this very fact. You may have a higher degree of holiness than I have, and I may have a higher degree of holiness than John Doe; however, by grace we are usable to our Lord to do his will while on we are on this earth. In other words, we are to do the work God has for us do and what He expects of us daily.

All female missionaries may not have the same holiness as Mother Theresa, but they can contribute to the missionary work as she has in her lifetime. All male pastors may not have the holiness of St. Paul, but they can with the Spirit and tend God's people as he wants them taught in their churches. I don't believe for one minute that we are to analyze whether one has more holiness than the other. I believe that is the Father, Son and Holy Spirit's work. I do believe that we are supposed to seek more of the Spirit's guidance in areas where we are not so holy. We are human beings and will not be perfected until the Lord returns to claim us for himself. Even when we are clothed with immortality, we will still be saved human sinners who by the grace of God alone have entered into eternity because he wanted us to be part of his eternal family. We will never be divine, just divinely loved and cared for by the Creator of the universe.

If you are a social media person or celebrity follower, holiness may not be something that interests you a great deal. In fact, you will probably never hear God's call. And if you do, it will be because of what the world thinks is good. If one such person does something for another, it may faintly resemble something godly or holy.

The biggest problem I see with society today is that we are all too selfish. It's all about me, and if you are in my way, watch out because I may run right over you. This part of society has become the victim if things are not going my way. I have been victimized! I have my rights! I demand to be compensated for my hurt! It's my right! Me, me, me. It's all about me.!

In Joshua, the Scriptures state that a country divided against itself will not stand. I believe that in the case of Quebec's separatist stance, and if indeed separation comes, Canada will not stand, allowing the opportunity for other interests to take over this nation.

All of the previous situations have absolutely nothing to do with being holy. In fact, it is because of ungodliness that these ideas and ideals have come about to begin with. When the ego takes the place of the I Am, you can see nothing but a downslide taking place—individually or governmentally.

If you are already a Christian, keep working out your holiness through the help of the Holy Spirit. Your salvation has already been sealed, and as Jesus mentions in the New Testament, you have passed from death into life eternal with your Lord. But for your holiness to abound, you will need all the help you can receive from the Holy Spirit. The Holy Spirit is always there to pick you up when you fail or when you fall. Try not to grieve the Holy Spirit and never compare the Spirit's work to that of Satan as some in the Bible have been accused of doing. That is the unpardonable sin, and you will never be forgiven this sin in this life or eternity. The Father, Son, and Holy Spirit are very holy spirits and can in no way be compared to Satan or any of Satan's works.

Satan may be allowed to cause you all kinds of trouble as he did Job in the Old Testament, but if you belong to God, Satan will never be able to destroy you. God will not let that happen. There have been many cases of people who are almost starving to death, call out to God, and receive his eternal blessings by coming to and acknowledging His Son, Jesus, the Savior of the world. Not all of us are destined to live in a five-bedroom home with a three-car garage all on an acre lot or earn a six-figure income year after year. God allows us to have what we can handle. So whatever your lot in life is, be holy because your Lord, God, and Savior is holy. Love the Lord, your God, with all your heart, your strength, and your mind.

Intercession

As defined in the *Bible Dictionary*, *intercession* is the art of petitioning God or praying on behalf of another person or group of persons.

Early in the Old Testament, Abram speaks to God on behalf of Sodom. His nephew, Lot, had chosen with his family to live in that city after their separation from Abraham because strife between Abraham and Lot's servants had developed over pasture land, etc. Wealth and acquisitions had created petty jealousies between Abraham and Lots' people. Sodom was not a good place, and sin of all kinds abounded in this city. God had warned Abraham that He was going to destroy the city and all of its inhabitants. Because Lot and his family lived there, Abraham pleaded with God not to destroy the city if the Lord found enough righteous people living there. God's angel led Lot, his wife, and his daughters out of the city before God rained down sulfur and fire from heaven to destroy the city. However, Lot's wife looked back and was changed into a pillar of salt.

Moses was another person who partitioned God by prayer on behalf of the Hebrew people. And when God humbled Pharaoh enough, he did let the Jews leave Egypt, and he asked Moses to pray to God for him and his people.

Because we are all sinners and live in an extremely sinful world, we all need an intercessor to pray to God on our behalf. The greatest intercession to take place is that of Jesus partitioning the Father for our forgiveness while he is seated by the right hand of God, having fulfilled the earthly duties that God required of him on our behalf.

If you are a Christian, the Holy Spirit continually intercedes on your behalf for the atonement of your sins. Unfortunately, though we have Christ as our Savior and Lord, we still need an intercessor for the sins that we continue to choose. Therefore, our bond with Jesus is the indwelling Holy Spirit, which knows us well and pleads with Jesus on our behalf because of our weaknesses to sin. As has been mentioned previously, we are not perfect individuals and will not put on immortality until the trumpet has sounded and God gathers his chosen from the earth.

Even though we are not perfect, God expects those of us who have claimed him as Lord and God to intercede on behalf of those who may not understand what they may be doing that is sinful and requires forgiveness by a heavenly Father, who is holy in every way.

There are many different reasons for interceding for a group, a person, or a place for God's protection, help, etc. I will only take time to mention some of those instances that have applied to me personally over the years.

When I was a younger person and not following any of God's ways, I was once informed by friends I had grown up with that the church they attended was praying for my salvation (coming to Christ). The community that I had grown up in knew my family well and also knew that we were very poor. They were concerned that if I didn't change or have Jesus in my heart, I would make many serious mistakes in life, and they didn't want to see that happen to me. My initial reaction to the community's concern for my well-being wasn't very positive. In fact, I was determined to show them that Al Paine would do as Al Paine pleased whether they liked it or not. Thank God—and I do thank God—that many of these friends, relatives, and neighbors continued to pray on my behalf. I don't know where I would be today or what I would be doing if God had left me alone and not intervened in the many areas of my life over the years.

There have been times in my life when I have been involved with others praying for an individual or family to receive God's grace by healing someone from a terrible disease that was bringing his or her life to ruin. Sometimes we pray after natural disasters like the recent tropical storm that devastated a large population in Philippines and wiped out many families and many homes, businesses, hospitals, etc. The Filipino people need much disaster aid and help to rebuild their communities and reestablish the community framework that existed before this enormous storm took place. Along with all the aid that will be supplied, the Filipino people also need your heartfelt prayers for God to help their people gain back their homes, livelihoods, hospitals, and services And, most of all we must continue thanking and praying to God for his hand in helping them through this horrible dilemma that they now find themselves in.

I pray even now that the Holy Spirit will intercede on behalf of the Filipino people and provide an effective missionary work to help those who have lost loved ones, homes, and everything that they had. As a North American who has had a fairly good life overall, I cannot fathom what many of these people's lives are like now or what they will be like in the future. I do believe that God, however, has a plan for each and every Filipino who has survived this disaster, and I pray that all of these people lean on God to find out exactly what he wants of them in this life. Seeing the horrendous devastating videos and news clips on the aftermath of this storm is very heartbreaking. I pray for an inner strength for the Filipino people not to give up on God because of this disaster that they have gone through. My understanding is that the Filipino people are very religious people. May their churches continue to promote God's will in their lives and even grow stronger in these perilous times we live in.

Pray with me that God allows no further storm or damage to come to one of the most beautiful places in the world as well as one with some of the most beautiful people in this world. May the Filipino people be restored and restructured as quickly as possible with all the aid that's possible to come and may words of praise to God sing out from all of the congregations that assemble in the Philippians in the future.

I sincerely pray for all of you who read these lines that the Lord has given me. If you are not a Christian, I pray that the Holy Spirit intercedes on your behalf to our Lord and Savior and that you accept Jesus into your life. If you are already a Christian, I pray that the Holy Spirit multiplies your witness to the Lord and that the gospel makes you much more fruitful in service to our Lord.

Servant

When we think of the word *servant*, we often associate it with slavery or occupation. We might think of a maid or butler who usually serves a wealthy individual or family. Or we might think of shoe repairmen or tailors who serve us in their work when we require their services.

However, I would like you to think of the service that Jesus did for us in regards to his Father's holy decree. Jesus was as Isaiah records in his writings, the servant of the Lord. He was the perfect servant, a sinless man who was also God. Jesus ministry was a serving ministry. He taught his disciples that they were to serve God by preaching the gospel to all—Jew, Gentile, free person, slave, male, female, rich, or poor. God has no room for partiality or favoritism. Jesus was the perfect role model for all of us.

Jesus was rejected by the people of his day because they were not prepared for a king that was willing to serve and give his life up without some sort of fight. They were expecting a messiah that would lead them into conquering their enemies in whatever way it took to do so. They (the Jews) also were not ready to hear that salvation would be received through his death on the cross for others (the Gentiles). They knew that Scripture had declared them as God's chosen people. And so they were, and so they are today. To serve or accept anyone other than a Jew was an offense and unthinkable for them. The servant Lord Jesus was not their king—or so they thought!

God knows man's heart, and he knew that the Jews would reject and demand Jesus crucifixion (death on the cross). Those of us who would be known as Gentiles can really appreciate Jesus' sacrifice as well as his teachings and further his calling of Paul to minister salvation to the Gentiles. Heaven's door has been opened ever since Jesus' ascension into heaven to reign at the right hand of the Father. With our belief in God providing a servant Savior, we will one day walk through heaven's door and into the Lord's glorious presence. Many of my immediate family members as well as many of my in-laws who have accepted Christ as their Savior and Lord are already there, and I can hardly wait for my time to join them. In the meantime I pray that I will serve the Lord here on earth better and better each day.

As described in the Scriptures, a servant's nature should be one of willingness to serve his or her master faithfully and to submit to his or her master's request. A servant should also have only one master because one cannot serve two masters faithfully. It would be impossible to please two masters equally in performing his or her duties.

Many of our police departments use the motto "To serve and protect," and this is an honorable ideal to have. I believe that most of the police force personnel sincerely intend to do exactly that when they join the various agencies. It is only when an individual or group of officers decide to take a few bribes and get involved with drug or criminal organizations that there is a breakdown of the "serve and protect" attitude. Moreover, once they have crossed over the line, it is very hard to get out of the problem they caused because they are indeed serving two masters. The Scripture is very clear on that point. You cannot serve two masters, and you will wind up hating one and loving the other if you try.

Thank God for all the police and policing organizations that have done a diligent and honorable job serving our country, communities, and God.

Although we are called to serve, we must also be sure of what and who we are serving. There are organizations and individuals who put up what is a good front, but we must research well anyone or any organization that attempts to get our service. God is not the only one who is recruiting servants. Satan is out there every day of the week on the street corners, bars, back alleys, and other places, selling his bill of goods to us as well. He obviously wants to lure as many individuals to serve in his way of life as possible. His time is short and growing shorter. He's going to lure away from God or godly ways as many people as he can. There is absolutely nothing good about Satan and any of his works.

He is a liar, a thief, and destroyer, and evil. However, don't forget that he is very powerful and the only way we are able to overcome Satan and his angels is through the power of our servant Lord Jesus Christ. Whenever you feel Satins attack call upon the name of the Lord and He will help you through the trials you may find yourself in.

Never forget that Satan is smart, that he is not stupid. He also feels that he is going to win the final battle against the Lord. But be assured that he will not. Remember and remind yourselves daily to serve the Lord, your God. He is the one and only one to serve, and he is our master as well. Try to remind yourself every day about the first two commandments—there is but one God, and we are to love the Lord with all of our heart soul and mind.

My prayer for you is that you indeed will come to know and serve the Lord and find a great deal of happiness in doing so. It might not be easy to do so. In fact, it is always much easier to serve the world, but there are no eternal blessings for serving the world or the Devil. God has promised in Scripture that if you give a cup of cold water to and individual, you will be rewarded in some way for doing so. Try to remember the Golden Rule, which says, "Do unto others as you would have them do unto you."

Second Coming

The *Bible Dictionary* states that the second coming is never expressly mentioned in Scripture. However, Christ's return is referred to more than three hundred times in the New Testament. Our Lord will return in the same manner he left. The angels at Jesus accession told the apostles this on his disappearance from their sight.

Indeed, his coming will be personal, bodily, and very visible. It will be a very climactic event. History will be complete for the Christian as he or she enters into eternal bliss with the Lord and Savior of mankind.

It is easy to get caught up into the setting of times for this event as it draws near. Many modern-day prophets are making millions on writing about this event with a new book, magazine, etc., available every week. Jesus tells us in Scripture that only the Father knows when this will take place. He alone will tell our Lord when he has had enough and wishes for Jesus to return and to gather his elect from the earth.

I believe that other than the Bible's description and explanation of the Lord's return, the video series *Left Behind* does a tremendous job in getting that message across to the everyday viewer, reader, or thinker. It is very clear that somewhere in the great tribulation to come,

Christ will return. I do believe that that time is very close at hand. We are seeing many earthquakes, tidal waves, fires, etc. Jesus describes these as a woman having labor pains. It certainly seems as though the earth is having great labor pains and is about to give birth to something that many of us may not live through. We may have no choice. We may live to see the so-called end of the earth as we know it. As in the *Left Behind* series, Christians are to resist any of the Devil's plans, lies, and actions. God doesn't want to lose anyone to Satan, and Satan will definitely know when the tribulation time is here. He will do all he can to destroy as many individuals as he can while he still has control of the earth and those who have rejected anything to do with God.

In the Scriptures we read where Israel will sign a peace treaty with her enemies halfway through this tribulation period. We see in the news all the time when other governments and their officials try to coerce Israel into not only signing a peace treaty now but also giving up even more land that they now claim as theirs. Once that treaty is signed, it will indeed be the beginning of the end. Scripture is very clear about the fact that halfway through this peacetime, war will break out, and it will be the worst time that people on the earth will ever know. It will be a war of wars!

In Corinthians 15, we read about the resurrected body. There are two types of bodies—the natural (human) body and the spiritual (heavenly) body. We are presently clothed with a decaying body of flesh and blood, but should we be alive at the last trumpet sound, we will be changed in a flash and given an imperishable spiritual body. I don't know about you, but I will be glad to eventually receive my imperishable spiritual body. In my seventy years on this earth, I have suffered with various diseases (some that have almost taken my life), broken bones, cuts, bruises, etc. Truly I have been blessed; however, when I see the tragic consequences of leprosy and other diseases that other people endure, I can only count my many blessing from our Lord, God, and Savior.

You might ask, "Why do I have to be concerned with the return of Christ anyway?" Well, if you do not belong to the Savior, you belong to the Devil. There is indeed a heaven, and there is indeed a hell. Before the return of Jesus, I would suggest that you commit to accepting Christ as your Savior and Lord and live according to God's Word. You and I are not perfect and will not be until God clothes us with an imperishable body, but we will be judged on what we have done in our flesh and blood. Jesus' return for his elect people will complete our salvation. We will be able to enter his presence. He will be our king. We may have lived in a country where there was a president, a prime minister, or a dictator, but Jesus will be our reigning king forever. His kingdom will not be temporary. It will be eternal.

We should watch, wait, and prepare for the great day. Once that day has come, we will receive our new bodies and be found blameless in the eyes of our God. We will also receive a crown to reign with our Lord and king. And somewhere in Scripture it states that we will be incredibly happy. I associate being incredibly happy with a permanent smile on my face. Won't that be something? It'll be a place where people smile, are happy, and want others to be happy as well. Certainly that's a far cry from the various dog-eat-dog societies that we live in today.

Jesus' return gets rid of all of that garbage. I'm looking forward to his second coming. I hope you are among those who are looking forward to his second coming too.

Election

Often when we think of the word *election*, we think of voting for a president, representative, prime minister, and/or others in government circles. In elections, we have choices about the candidates we vote for and the various platforms that they stand for.

In the biblical sense of election, we are chosen by God to be his people by accepting the Son, Jesus Christ, as our Savior and Lord. To be among the elect is a great blessing to us from God, for it is by his grace alone that we are chosen, not by any works, money, or status that we may have in a given society. God prefers for all mankind to be saved, but he knew from day one that many would reject him and be forever lost.

Many people have been often heard murmuring about the Jewish people and their chosen status as a nation by God. Indeed, over the years many Jews have rejected God and failed in the service to him as their sovereign God. In fact, many still deny today that Jesus is their Messiah and are still looking for the Messiah to come. The fact remains that God has never and never will forget that Israel is his chosen people and indeed will be the leaders in his future priesthood to come in the new heaven and new earth. When you read the Holy Scriptures, you will come to realize that salvation was first meant for the Jews and that by their rebelling against our God, we were given the blessing of receiving God's grace and salvation through belief in gis one and only Son.

I don't know about you, but I feel very happy to be called a son of God. After the fall of Adam mankind was condemned as sinners, and therefore, we needed a way to get back into the graces of God. Jesus Christ is that way, the truth, and the life. Only through Him are we redeemable to God.

If you find yourself thinking that you are not good enough to come to God, *stop doing that!* You will never be good enough to come to God. Nor will anyone else. There was only one perfect person in the world, and that was God's only begotten Son, Jesus Christ. If you hear his call to you, don't put him off. He wants to work in you to glorify the Father. There are many so-called good people, but if they haven't accepted Christ as their Savior and Lord, they are doomed sinners. *Do not join them!*

Predestination is another term that goes along with election. God has chosen you or me or anyone else that He chooses to share eternity with Him. He knows us in and out and realizes all of our weaknesses and faults. Once he has chosen you, you should submit to his every will for you in this life. It is for his glory that you have been elected to share in eternal salvation with others God has predestined to share eternal life with him. He will surely see you through this life and into eternity. Praise him for all you are worth. Remember always that he did not have to choose you. He chose to choose you. Be glad and happy about that.

You may have heard, as I have, the many times people have said, "I can't buy into this Christ thing. I don't believe in God." The truth is that you can't buy or purchase God. He is not for sale! Truth cannot be bought for a price. God is truth. Those who feel there must be a price on something like God have missed the whole point totally.

If you must put a price on your relationship to God and you are one of his elect, ask him to increase your faith, for it is by faith that you were chosen by him to begin with. He chose you as you were, no matter how rich or poor, whether you are black or white, good or bad, high or low. He took you as you were at the moment he revealed himself to you. He could easily have said, "Don't want that one." Allow him to use your every being and serve him as your sovereign king because that is what he is. And one day, hopefully soon, he will return and set up his glorious kingship here on earth and rule eternally.

I don't know about you, but I can hardly wait for that moment to come.

The Bible teaches us that when we have the assurance that we are one of God's elect, we have certain responsibilities to go along with that. We are to act on our faith and even ask God for more faith as many in the Bible have done long before us. We are also to be assured of our salvation and continually praise the Lord for granting us that salvation. He will help us be more like our Savior, who died for us so that we could be saved from our wretched state. We are to do good works and bear fruit by witnessing to others about Christ and what he has done for us.

If others see Christ working in our lives, it may encourage them to explore some of the feelings that we may be portraying to them.

You never know what a kind word or act may do to bring someone to Christ. Try to always be aware of your surroundings and praise God in everything that comes your way.

Righteousness

As described in the *Bible Dictionary*, *righteousness* is holy and upright living in accordance to God's standard. God's character is the definitive source of all righteousness.

In the context of relationships, righteous action is action that promotes peace and well-being of human beings in their relationships to one another.

Homosexuality is an unrighteous act that the world wants you to accept as the standard for modern-day living. God's wrath stands against this practice whether performed by men or women. It was the cause of divine judgment against Sodom and Gomorrah. It will be the reason for many people worldwide to eventually experience God's wrath. It will also be the downfall of many societies that have openly endorsed the acceptance of homosexual behavior. It is an act that goes against God's righteous standard for everyday living, and it is a sin, not a sickness as many would have you to believe.

In Canada the so-called rates of homosexually are between 1 to 2 percent, according to a recent internet query. I believe it is much higher than that for the following reasons: Government offices are full of homosexuals and information about having to accept homosexuality. Municipal offices are the same. Schools are loaded with homosexuals, and the military turns a blind eye to this type of behavior as well. Many families have a son or daughter who has come out of the closet, and many churches accept homosexual behavior. We have a very serious problem on our hands, and watching TV, reading the newspaper, or going online will not solve the problem. Instead, these areas of society promote a homosexual lifestyle as being okay.

Well, homosexuality is not okay. It never has been of God's intent for mankind. It is not now God's intent for mankind, and it never will be God's intent for mankind. We are to avoid homosexuality and anyone or anything to do with it. Yet we are bombarded with it every day, and many more people are accepting that lifestyle.

I've heard people present arguments that Jesus had a homosexual relationship with the apostle John. I don't for one minute accept that premise, and I never will. My Lord and Savior would not and will not accept that type of behavior from anyone. He may very well forgive someone's sins in that regard, but he will never accept that lifestyle.

There are also those who would argue that in order to be righteous, you have to accept one's homosexuality for his or her well-being because that is what righteousness stands for—one's well-being. That is only an argument proposed by people in authority trying to whitewash God's standard of righteousness. Righteousness in not righteousness if it accepts unrighteous behavior. You may have to live amongst those who adhere to a homosexual lifestyle, but you do not have to accept it in your heart or your own lifestyle. The law may say you have to accept this lifestyle, but you do not have to accept homosexuality in your heart or being as an acceptable way to live. If you truly believe that Jesus Christ is the Son of God, you are credited with Christ's righteousness. Jesus' righteousness is a gift from God and leads a believer to salvation. Though one believes in Christ, it doesn't make the act of any unrighteousness behavior acceptable to God. Yes, Jesus may forgive us of any unrighteous acts—and thank God that he does and has become the mediator for us to the Father—but to trample on the Lord's righteousness to perform unrighteous acts is not acceptable behavior. Turn away from all unrighteousness acts and seek God's guidance in your everyday affairs and everyday living. Be holy because your God is holy. Obviously seek forgiveness for any unrighteousness acts that you may have committed or commit and ask for more guidance from the Holy Spirit to help you on the right track. Seek God! He is only a prayer away.

Voice

The *Bible Dictionary* doesn't give a definition of voice as such. But is does give a very descriptive definition of the Word of God, which I will use in this section and try to tie together with the Bible's commentaries on voice.

In both the Old Testament as well as in the New Testament, the human voice is described as the communication of information from one individual to another. We also use our voices to identify those we wish to speak to, give directions, etc. For instance, I may recognize a guy at work who knows someone I want to get a message to and ask him, "Hey, Joe, would you see that John gets this message? I won't be here to give it to him. Thanks."

A minister uses his voice to preach a sermon that he has prepared for worship service and may lead us into prayer during that worship service using his voice as well. Our voices can be expressed in many different ways. A traffic cop may shout at someone, "Don't cross the street till I have the vehicles all stopped." Or protestors may use complaining voices toward a subject or movement that they disagree with. When a tragic event has taken place, you may hear the sound of a weeping voice expressing deep sorrow for what has happened to them or someone close to them.

The Bible describes God's voice as sometimes being accompanied by fire or thunder and even as a gentle whisper at times.

When the Lord talked to Moses, he first talked to him from a burning bush and told Moses to remove his sandals because he was on holy ground. When Samuel was a small boy, God talked to him in a gentle whisper and gave Samuel instructions to give to Eli, the priest.

God's voice affirmed many things in the Bible through various prophets and religious individuals. Moses received the Ten Commandments on Mt. Sinai, which were given to him directly from God. John received the Word of God affirming Jesus as his only begotten Son after John had baptized Jesus in the Jordan River.

As God's subjects here on earth, we have the responsibility of recognizing God's voice, listening to his voice, and finally obeying his voice. God's voice leads to life eternally. Jesus identifying with the Father made it clear to the apostles and others that he was the way, the truth, and the life. By Jesus and Jesus alone, one will find the way, be given the complete truth, and receive eternal life to dwell forever with the greatest person who ever walked this earth.

Jesus Christ, our Savior and Lord, is the true Word of God. In the *Bible Dictionary*, he is described as God's divine agent in the creation of the universe. By the Word (voice) of God, the heavens were made.

Jesus is the means by which God makes himself known, declares his will for our being, and brings about his purposes for and in our lives.

Jesus brought to this world the personal presence of God. He was God in the flesh. His Word meets the deep human needs of every heart. One can feel very secure by following the teachings of our Lord and Savior, Jesus Christ. When you have the time to meditate, listen for that inner voice directing you as Jesus would have you walk in your time left on this earth. After all, he owns everything in the universe, and we are his as well. With your own voice, always praise the name of Jesus and keep a great deal of reverence for that name.

Inheritance

As described in the *Bible Dictionary*, *inheritance* is the receipt of property as a gift or by legal right usually upon the death of one's father.

In the ancient past tribal customs would rule as to how the distribution of property of a deceased individual was to be handled. There weren't wills as we know them today. Usually the older son would receive a double share of the estate. He was to take care of his mother and unwed sisters within the family. This is why he would receive the double portion allotted to him. The tribe was responsible for seeing that the deceased property would be divided up according to their customs. The tribal rules were followed very closely to see that any property that belonged to the tribe stayed in the tribe.

Later the Greeks relied on wills similar to what we have today. However, the major portions of the estates were divided between the male heirs of the family. If no male heir was living, it was passed on to the daughters. If a man died and left no natural heir, his property would go to his closest living relative.

Roman law divided the property of a deceased person without a will between the wife and the children. If the individual had no natural heirs but had adopted a son or daughter, the property would then go to that individual. But as with the Greeks, if a person died and left no natural heir, his closest relative would receive his property as an inheritance. Legally adopted children also had full inheritance right to a deceased person's property.

In the Scriptures Paul's concept of spiritual inheritance was primarily based on Jewish origin but greatly influenced by the Greeks and Romans. Firstly inheritance was regarded as immediate as well as ultimate. Secondly all legitimate heirs shared the inheritance equally. And thirdly legally adopted children shared full inheritance rights.

We are all sons of God through our faith in Jesus Christ. The Spirit's indwelling power seals us as heirs of God's promise. All of us who are redeemed become God's adopted sons with full inheritance rights.

What do we inherit by becoming God's sons and daughters? Well, this is spelled out in the various Scriptures in the Bible. We inherit the earth, the kingdom of heaven, the kingdom of light, the kingdom of God, eternal life, everything. Please don't worry if you are poor here on earth. You will be extremely wealthy when you go on to be with the Lord. He owns everything.

How do we know this? It is in the Scriptures. Gen 1:1 That's good enough for me. It is given by God and his Word. It is received as a reward. It is kept in heaven. It is imperishable. It is eternal. It is guaranteed by the Spirit, but it can be lost through disobedience.

More than two thousand years have passed by since Jesus walked this earth's surface. Many didn't want to listen to his message then, and many do not want to listen to his message now. Two thousand years is a short time compared to eternity. I don't know about you, but I'm looking forward to sharing eternal life with those believers in my family, friends, and associates who have gone on to their resting place till Christ returns to redeem the rest of us.

Jew I am not. Gentile I am. However, either way I will be an adopted son of God, and that's all I care about. I do hope that many of you who read this writing come to a spiritual fulfillment and learn that you are a son or daughter of God and that you will be entering eternity to be with your Lord and Savior, Jesus Christ. May the words of your mouth and mediations of your heart be acceptable to the Lord God, your friend and mine.

Courage

As defined in the *Bible Dictionary*, *courage* is the strength of purpose that enables one to withstand fear or difficulty. Physical courage is based on moral courage—a reliance on the presence and power of God and a commitment to his commandments.

The Bible also indicates that courage is the ability to face danger without fear. Many stories that are told in the Bible illustrate enormous courage by God's chosen individuals in performance of their God-given duties. Some examples include Moses confronting Pharaoh, David confronting Goliath, Daniel surviving in the lions' den, and Saul (Paul) preaching in Damascus.

Before Paul met Jesus on the road to Damascus, he had been responsible for arresting, jailing, and approving of the murders of many Jewish converts to Christianity. Obviously Paul was a man for the new Christians to fear. He was on his way to Damascus to arrest, jail, and have others killed in the area for following the way of Jesus.

When Jesus met Paul on the way, he directed Paul to follow him and minister to the Gentiles for the Lord. Paul didn't hesitate to do as he was told. He must have had a great deal of courage and faith that the Lord would see him safely into his new ministry, where he had been persecuting God's people for sometime before the Lord would meet him on the road to Damascus. Paul's ministry was very successful, and the Lord kept him from hurt for a very long time. Paul is also responsible for a great deal of the New Testament writings.

There were many commands in the Bible to be courageous. Some examples of these commands include Moses to the Israelites, when leaving Egypt, Solomon from David, when taking his place as king of Israel, the disciples from Jesus, Paul from the Lord, and to all of us as well. I believe that we all realize that it takes courage to face any danger or difficulty and to face what the future may bring as well. The question that remains is this: Where do we find that courage?

The source of all courage is to be found in God the Father, Jesus Christ, and the Holy Spirit. The Trinity is our all-in-all courage giver. Asking for and being given courage to help you through any problem or task is a divine blessing. Do not hesitate to ask the Lord for his help. He is always there for you and will never let you down.

One of my favourite passages in the Scriptures regarding courage is Psalm 23, which says at ome point, "Yea though I walk through the valley of the shadow of death, I will fear no evil." Why would the psalmist be so courageous? Because he had the Lord on his side and knew he would not fail. This same courage can be yours and mine if we ask for it.

Eternal

Eternity is infinite and unlimited, a time without beginning or end. Eternal life then is a person's redeemed existence that is granted by God through his Son, Jesus Christ.

Everlasting life is found in the Old Testament in the book of Daniel. New Testament references to eternal life are found primarily relating to a future orientation. Only in the book of John is there any emphasis on present reality of the eternal life of Christians.

Taking as literal Jesus' words that God's kingdom came with him on earth, I tend to identify with John. In a word, we passed from death to life once we became believers. We will surely die, but once dead to this earthly body of skin, blood, and bones, we go into an eternal realm and will be clothed with our heavenly bodies. I also believe that we have already been judged at that point, and the blessing that will come with a new spiritual body will be in an eternal home in heaven. We will have an eternal inheritance and live in an eternal kingdom forever and ever.

As has been mentioned previously, Christ will be our reigning king with all the authority that the Father gives him. He will be in complete control and will rule as we have never experienced rule in our lifetime.

I don't know about you, but I don't believe that we will sit around idle all day long in heaven, if indeed there are days as we know them now. I do believe that Jesus will have an assigned task for each and every one of us.

However, there will be no aches or pain in heaven, and that's one thing I'm looking forward to. Christ himself will wipe away all tears. What a faithful, loving, heavenly Lord who will make us feel at home.

Summary

In using my initial outline for this writing—life in his service—I hope that you have been brought to the understanding that there is indeed one God the Father, Christ the Son, and the Holy Spirit. These three make up the Trinity of the Godhead.

I also hoped you learned that God has eternity in mind for all of us. We are free to accept him or reject him, but he will have his way with all of us—one way or another.

I hope you have discovered in this writing that salvation is based on belief in Christ, the only begotten Son of God, being born of a virgin, dying on the cross, rising three days later, and ascending to heaven to be with the Father until his second coming to redeem those of us who have believed in Him.

The Bible is loaded with stories and examples of those who have been martyred for Christ's sake. But from Genesis to Revelation, God wants you to know that he loves you and wants you to come to him and receive eternal life through faith and belief in his Son, Jesus, whose blood was shed for all of our sins.

Whether you agree with my writing or disagree with it, my hope is that you will desire to research the

Scriptures for yourself and come to know more about the Creator of the universe. I also hope that you have come to learn that we are not just evolutionary beings that by chance developed eventually into humans but that we were created by God in his image.

May our Lord and God increase your desire to serve him every day in one form or another. He alone is your great reward. Love him as you have never loved anyone or anything else in your entire life on this earth. And always remember to worship him and not his created things.

Sources

KJV, the Holy Bible, World Publishing Company, Cleveland and New York

NIV, *Study Bible*, Zondervan Publishing, Grand Rapids, Michigan, USA

Nelsons, *Bible Dictionary*, Nashville, Dallas, Mexico City, used for clarifying biblical terms

Newspaper and media articles, used for clarifying current issues cited in writings.

Other Works by Alvino Paine

Jesus is Coming, album, Xuan Recordings

Al's Favorite Gospel and Country Songs, Xuan Recordings

Come to Me, Xuan Recordings

All these recordings available on iTunes or Amazon, and they are occasionally played on SongCastRadio.com